The Climber's World

STACKPOLE
BOOKS

WE SUPPORT TIBETAN PEOPLE

Welcome to our second book of mountain photography, which is even more special than the first, because as with any publishing adventure we weren't sure at the outset that there would be another.

During this past year we have continued our visual journey through the thousands of amazing photos we received from photographers around the globe.

Through this thoroughly enjoyable process, we have found the image to be a magic crucible.

Photos contain fluid messages that go beyond borders, differences in

E D I T O R I A L

languages, races, traditions and religions. Through this medium it also provides an important opportunity to share an impetus to respect and protect our mountains.

New sections have been added to this edition: the four elements of air, water, earth, and fire; flora and fauna, and a glimpse at the characters who chose to live in the mountains. The new themes reveal fresh stories that have flowed together thanks to this common language of photography. Combined, this helps form the basis of our passion for the mountains.

We'd like to take this opportunity to welcome new friends in this unique chorus, photographers from England, Australia, Japan, Spain and Finland.

And thanks to you, the readers, who have allowed us to continue. You have chosen to share with us a spectrum of emotions that range from fatigue and suffering to plain and simple joy.

We sincerely hope that mountains will continue to act as the catalyst and will bring you peace and serenity at the dawn of this millenium.

Betta and Gioachino

We would like to continue
this dialogue with the mountains
through your images,
so if anybody
is interested please get in touch.

Grivelart - Betta Gobbi - P.O. Box 76
- 11013 Courmayeur (AO) - Italy.
Phone: 0039.0165.843714
Fax: 0039.0165.844800
Email: grivelart@grivel.com

CONTENTS

Peaks

Cime

Cimes

Gipfel

Cimas

P   E   A   K   S

Kaga Pamari
and Kaga Tondo
(approximately 1000 m),
Mali, Africa,
Ph. Ray Wood.

Shivling (6543 m),
India,
Ph. Laurence Gouault.

Aiguille Plan (3672 m),
Mt. Blanc (4810 m),
Chamonix,
France,
Ph. Dietmar Walser.

Stefan Siegrist
approaching
Cerro Torre (3128 m),
Argentina,
Ph. Thomas Ulrich.

Mt. Kailash
and lake Manasarovar,
picture taken
from the summit of Mt.
Gurla Mandata (7500 m),
Tibet,
*Ph. Expedition
Gurla Vertical.*

Torres del Paine (2460 m),
Chile,
Ph. Heinz Zak.

Mt. Nuptse (7833 m),
Himalaya, Nepal,
Ph. Vadem Nevorotin.

K2 (8611 m) seen from
the air
over the Baltoro Glacier,
Pakistan,
Ph. Galen Rowell.

Mt. Rathong (6679 m),
Yalung Glacier,
Kangchenjunga area,
Nepal,
Ph. Klepinin Arkadi.

Gasherbrum's serac,
Gasherbrum (8068 m),
Pakistan,
Ph. Sergio De Leo.

Cotopaxi (5897 m),
Equador,
Ph. Patrick Wagnon.

Matterhorn (4478 m),
Felikpass,
Italian Alps,
Ph. Davide Camisasca.

Mt. Rainier (4392 m)
and Reflexion Lake,
Mt. Rainier National Park,
USA,
Ph. Tuan Luong.

Grand Teton (4282 m),
Wyoming,
USA,
Ph. Laurent Bouvet.

Earth	*Terra*	*Terre*	*Erde*	*Tierra*
Water	*Acqua*	*Eau*	*Wasser*	*Agua*
Wind	*Vento*	*Vent*	*Wind*	*Viento*
Fire	*Fuoco*	*Feu*	*Feuer*	*Fuego*

E A R T H

W A T E R

W I N D

F I R E

Appenzell,
Switzerland
Ph. Peter Mathis.

Acacous,
Bia-Sahara, Africa,
Ph. Mario Verin.

Roussillon,
France,
Ph. Wilfried Zwaans.

Canyon del Muerto,
USA,
Ph. Gérard Kosicki.

Merced River,
Yosemite National Park,
California, USA,
Ph. Peter Mathis.

Sihl Valley,
Switzerland,
Ph. Rainer Eder.

Piave River seen
from Pian di Coltura,
Italy,
*Ph. Giandomenico
Vincenzi.*

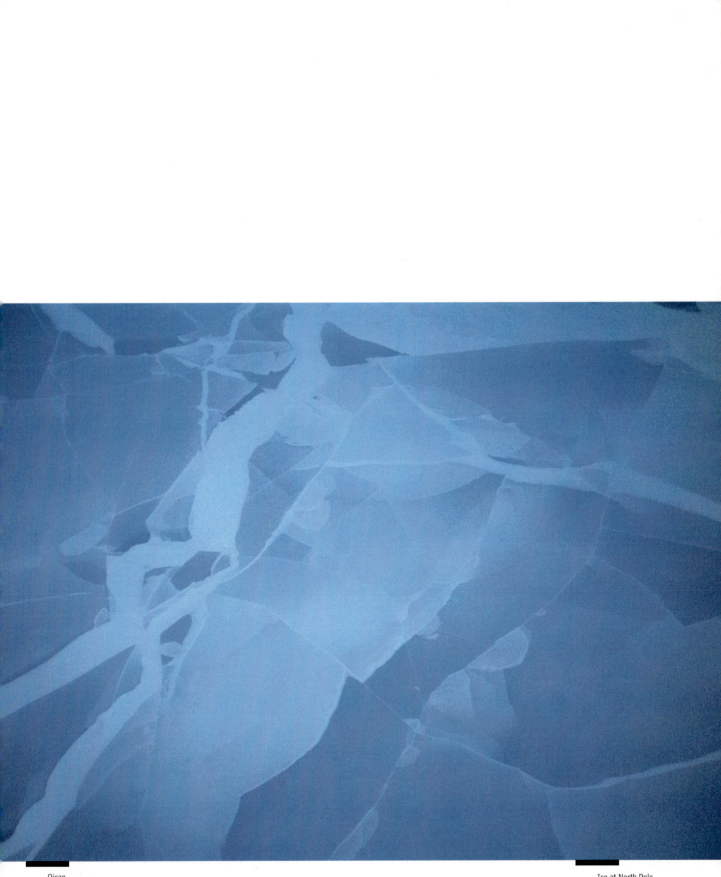

Oisan,
Romancho Valley,
France,
Ph. Gérard Kosicki.

Ice at North Pole,
Ph. Borge Ousland.

Yellowstone basins,
Yellowstone National Park,
Wyoming,
USA,
Ph. Marco Scolaris.

Castle Geyser,
Yellowstone National
Park,
Wyoming,
USA,
Ph. Peter Mathis.

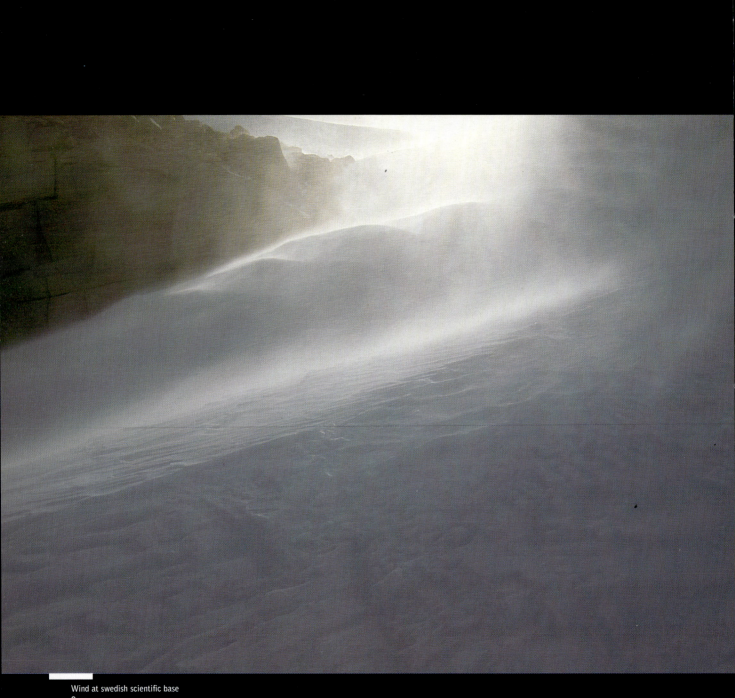

Wind at swedish scientific base
Svea,
Dronning Maud Land,
Antarctica,
Ph. Anders Modig.

Backfire management,
Yosemite National Park,
USA,
Ph. Tuan Luong.

Fauna *Fauna* *Fauna* *Fauna* *Fauna*

Flora *Flora* *Flora* *Flora* *Flora*

F A U N A

F L O R A

Butterfly on the hand
of Stefan Siegrist,
Bernese Oberland,
Switzerland,
Ph. Thomas Ulrich.

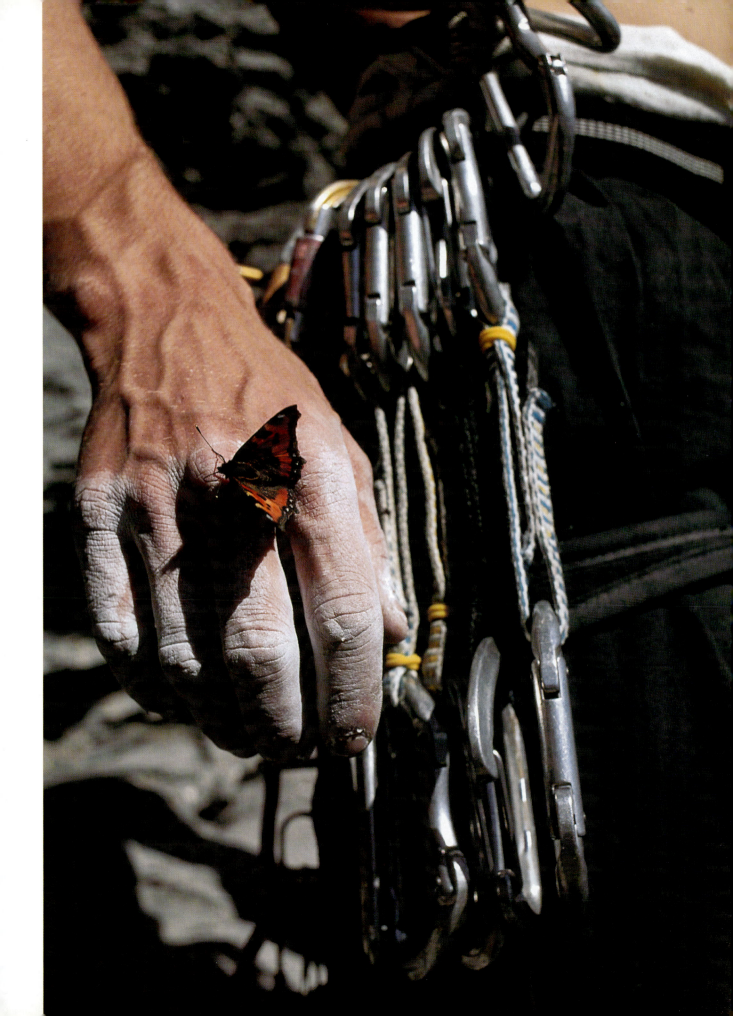

Blue sheep on slopes,
Mt. Kangchenjunga
north base camp,
East Nepal,
Ph. Pat Morrow.

Raven wing prints,
Kahiltna Glacier,
Alaska, USA,
Ph. Galen Rowell.

Dead trees
on the way to
Mt. Fitz Roy,
Patagonia, Argentina,
Ph. Robert Bösch.

Red Rock,
Las Vegas,
Nevada Desert,
USA,
Ph. Uli Wiesmeier.

Deer at sunset,
Sierra Màgina, Jaèn,
Spain,
Ph. David Munilla.

Chipmunk, Zion
National Park,
USA,
Ph. Klaus Fengler.

Larch cone,
Livrio Valley, Sondrio,
Italy,
Ph. Federico Raiser.

Mountain lion in snow,
Montana, USA,
Ph. Daniel J. Cox.

Goshawk feeding
its birdies,
Balcani mts, Greece,
Ph. Gian Luca Boetti.

Mushrooms
Lentiai,
Belluna Valley, Italy,
*Ph. Giandomenico
Vincenzi.*

Slugs mating,
Italian Alps,
Ph. Cesare Cossavella.

Guadiaro, Spain,
Ph. David Munilla.

Yaks under the snow
on the way to
Mt. Shishapangma,
Tibet,
Ph. Philippe Rebreyend.

Goats at Piani
di Bobbio,
Italy,
Ph. Federico Raiser.

R O C K

C L I M B I N G

Dean Potter
on "Thank God Ledge"
Regular Route, 5.11 A2
soloing Half Dome
NorthWest Face, USA,
Ph. Heinz Zak.

Ben Moon,
Cornalba,
Italy,
Ph. Robert Bösch.

Patrick Edlinger
bouldering
on Hueco Tanks,
Texas, USA,
Ph. Gérard Kosicki.

Mike Talbot on
"Scorched Earth", 5.12 A
Jumbo Rock,
Joshua Tree, USA,
Ph. Guillaume Vallot.

Jean-Christophe Lafaille
and Emosson Dam,
longest artificial climbing
route in the world,
France,
Ph. Philippe Poulet.

Yuji Hirayama,
Climbing World Cup,
Milano, Italy,
Ph. Marco Scolaris.

Andrew Dunbar
attempting "Monkey Puzzle",
The Gallery,
The Grampians, Victoria,
Australia,
Ph. Simon Carter.

Chris Harmston,
"Fat Cat" with moon,
Indian Creek Canyon,
Utah, USA,
Ph. Kennan Harvey.

Roxanne Wells on
"The Free Route",
The Totem Pole, Cape Hauy,
Tasmania, Australia,
Ph. Simon Carter.

Stephan Matholin,
And then there was…,
Sardinia, Italy,
Ph. Gérard Kosicki.

McLeod and Kirsty
Hamilton,
"Passport to Insanity",
The Fortress, The
Grampians, Victoria,
Australia,
Ph. Simon Carter.

Alex Huber
and Gerhard Hörhager
supporting a Bavarian
climbing lady,
Schleier waterfall, Tirol,
Austria,
Ph. Heinz Zak.

Laurence Gouault
and Stevie Haston,
Ancient Art,
Fisher Towers, USA,
Ph. Stevie Haston.

Christian Frick,
7a+, St. Blasien,
Black Forest, Germany,
Ph. Rainer Eder.

Johannes Schlemper,
Bouldertraining
"Hyperdynamo",
Zürich, Switzerland,
Ph. Klaus Fengler.

Stefan Glowacz
and Wolfgang Widder
on "Schweizer Weg",
Westwall of Lavaredo,
Dolomites, Italy,
Ph. Gerd Heidorn.

"Halloween",
Baback Kiampour,
"Chain Reaction",
5.12c Smith Rock,
USA,
Ph. Sam Bié.

Alberto Gnerro
bouldering on Lys Col,
Susa Valley, Italy,
Ph. Andrea Gallo.

Mario Verin
on Bandiagara Cliff
climbing with the tipical
ladder used
by the Dogon Tribe,
Mali, Africa,
Ph. Mario Verin.

Cathérine Destivelle
on Bandiagara Cliff
discovering an ancient
cimitery of
the Dogon Tribe,
Mali, Africa,
Ph. Gérard Kosicki.

François Legrand
yawning at full moon,
Boux, France,
Ph. Uli Wiesmeier.

Christian Lupiòn on
"Explosiòn duradera", 8a,
Los Vados, Spain,
Ph. David Munilla.

I C E

C L I M B I N G

Christophe Moulin
on "Rappelle-toi
que tu es un homme",
Hautes-Alpes, France,
Ph. Manu Molle.

Alex Huber on
"Klammbaam", grade 6,
Partnachklamm,
Wetterstein, Germany,
Ph. Heinz Zak.

Gregor Seitz on
an icefall
in Argentière,
France,
Ph. Klaus Fengler.

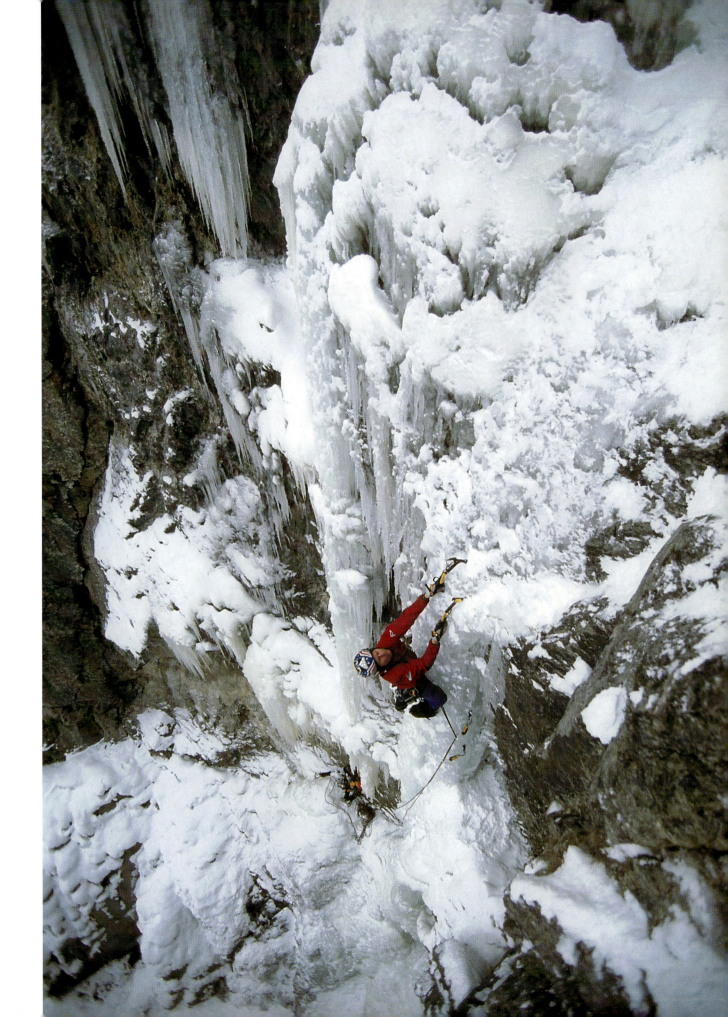

Beni Fahner on
Godwin Austen Glacier,
Karakorum, Pakistan,
in the back: K2,
Ph. Robert Bösch.

Bruno Gardont,
Crevasse's exploration,
Glacier de la Meije,
France,
Ph. Laurent Bouvet.

Jérome Blanc Gras on
"Résurgence",
Fournel, France,
Ph. J. Blanc Gras.

Structure of the
Iceclimbing Competition
Cortina,
Dolomites, Italy,
Ph. Manu Ibarra.

Train, Affiche
Kirov, Russia,
Ph. Manu Ibarra.

Ildi Kiss,
Iceclimbing Competition
Cortina, Dolomites, Italy,
Ph. Manu Ibarra.

Sami Saleva
on "Mammuth fall",
Korouoma, Posio,
Finland,
Ph. Sauli Herva.

Cathérine Destivelle
on 0.5 Gully,
Ben Nevis, Scotland,
Ph. Erik Decamp.

Stefan Glowacz
and Jürgen Knappe,
Mt. Zugspitze, Germany,
Ph. Gerhard Heidorn.

Alpinism   Alpinismo   Alpinisme   Alpinismus   Alpinismo

A L P I N I S M

Mark Stewart
ascent of Pigeon Spire
west ridge, Bugaboo
Prov. Park, B.C. Canada,
Ph. Pat Morrow.

Westface Latok II,
background
Nanga Parbat,
Alex Huber
resting in the portaledge,
Ph. Thomas Huber.

Alpinists Ascending
Mt. Blanc,
in the background
Grand Mulet,
Ph. Sylvie Chappaz.

Alpinists
at Tarfala, Kebnekaise,
North Sweden,
Ph. Anders Modig.

Mt. Matterhorn,
North face,
"Le Grand Voyage",
Jean-Christophe Lafaille,
Switzerland,
Ph. Philippe Poulet.

Mt. Annapurna,
South face,
Cathérine Destivelle,
Nepal,
Ph. Erik Decamp.

Leif Patterson at Urdukas,
Karakorum, Himalaya,
K2 Expedition
Ph. Galen Rowell.

Mt. Kusmkangur,
East face 1st ascent on solo,
Nepal,
Yasushi Yamanoi,
Ph. Yasushi Yamanoi

Couzy Demaison, North
face Mt. Olan,
France (sous l'orage),
Anne Bauvois,
Ph. Frédéric Hasbani.

Mer de Glace,
Chamonix, France,
Alex and Thomas Huber,
Ph. Uli Wiesmeier.

C H A R A C T E R S

Karin and Pepi,
Goisern, Austria,
Ph. Leo Himsl.

El Bao,
Falesina, Pergine
Valsugana, Trentino, Italy,
Ph. Flavio Faganello.

Mirjam Verbeek,
Amsterdam,
The Netherlands,
Ph. Wilfried Zwaans.

Antoine Le Menestrel,
La Baume Rousse,
France,
Ph. Wilfried Zwaans.

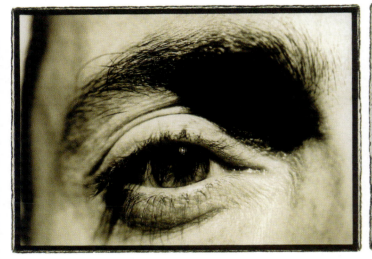

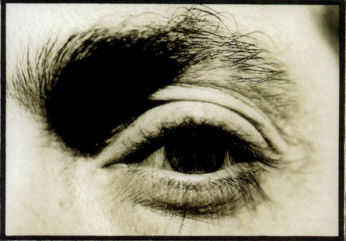

J.B. Tribout, right eye,
Pertuis, France,
Ph. Wilfried Zwaans.

J.B. Tribout, left eye,
Pertuis, France,
Ph. Wilfried Zwaans.

White Fang Film Set,
Alaskan Brown Bear,

Mountain guide during
Mid-Summer
Mountain guide Festival,
Chamonix, France,
Ph. Xavier Murillo.

A farmer in the cave
of Archidona,
Hoya del Guadalorce,
Málaga, Spain,
Ph. David Munilla.

Chestnuts picker,
Arnad,
Aosta Valley,
Ph. Cesare Cossavella.

Husband and wife,
Casteltesino, Valsugana,
Trentino, Italy,
Ph. Flavio Faganello.

Berber shepherd,
Tador, Morocco,
Ph. David Munilla.

Children playing
with expedition drums,
Tengpoche,
Solu Khumbu, Nepal,
Ph. Xavier Murillo.

Francesco Fedele
(paleoanthropologist),
San Giacomo Valley,
Central Alps, Italy,
Ph. Gian Luca Boetti.

Goisern man,
Goisern, Austria,
Ph. Leo Himsl.

Balti porters at moon rise,
Concordia, K2,
Pakistan,
Ph. Bill O'Connor.

Selfportrait,
Akarkhar Valley,
Pamir,
Ph. Sergei Savchenko.

Life *Vita* *La Vie* *Leben* *Vida*

L I F E

Santner peak,
Siusi Alps,
Dolomites, Italy,
Ph. Giandomenico Vincenzi.

Christmas in wilderness
(-40°C),
Inari, Finland,
Ph. Sauli Herva.

Porters warming
themselves in front
of the fire,
Manali, India,
Ph. Philippe Rebreyend.

Young shepherd with gun,
Majunla Pass,
Tibet,
Ph. Davide Camisasca.

Dogon fortune-teller,
Mali, Africa,
Ph. Mario Verin.

Wooden hut,
Mt. Civetta,
Dolomites, Italy,
Ph. Marco Scolaris.

Peter Bauer
snowboarding in front of
Neuschwanstein castle,
Bavaria, Germany,
Ph. Peter Mathis.

Women washing
hand painted fabrics,
Gangotri, India,
Ph. Manrico Dall'Agnola.

Shepherd with his flock,
Bettmeralp, Wallis,
Switzerland,
Ph. Robert Bösch.

Typical straw huts,
Somiedo Natural Park,
Asturias, Spain,
Ph. Eduardo Velasco.

Bame Guelle Dinwelle
village with Hand of Fatima
in the background,
Mali, Africa,
Ph. Ray Wood.

C H A O S

Radical Ski-track,
Schilthorn,
Bernese Oberland,
Switzerland,
Ph. Thomas Ulrich.

Unité de Reconnaissance
Humaine 27, 93ème
Régiment d'Artillerie
de Montagne,
Armée de Terre, France,
Ph. Phillippe Poulet.

Equipe montagne, 13ème
Régiment de Dragons
Parachutistes/Dieuze,
Brigade de
Renseignement,
Armée de Terre, France,
Ph. Phillippe Poulet.

Entrance to the
Mt. Blanc tunnel, Italy,
Ph. Xavier Murillo.

Cable car wires,
Belledonne Massif,
France,
Ph. Gérard Kosicki.

Ropes on the
Kinshofer Route,
Nanga Parbat,
Pakistan,
Ph. Laurence Gouault.

Ice avalanche,
Albula, Switzerland,
Ph. Marco Milani.

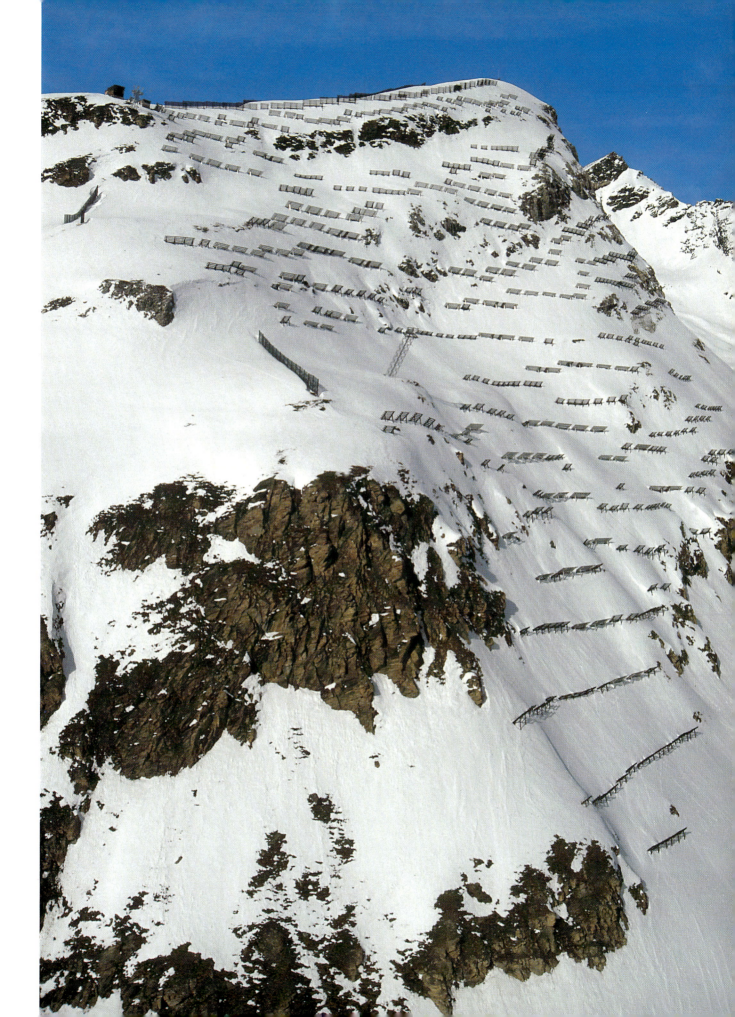

Topher Donahue
with altitude
uneasiness, Mt. Neacola,
Alaska, USA,
Ph. Kennan Harvey.

Bicho Fiorenza
rescued by
Carlo Micheli,
east face of Cerro
Torre, Argentina,
Ph. Bruno Sourzac.

Claudio Monticola
attempting
Mt. Cho Oyu,
Tibet,
Ph. Philippe Rebreyend.

Unexploded bomb,
Simplon col, Switzerland,
Ph. Patrick Gabarrou.

Mt. Kailas painted

S P I R I T

The Holy Man
"Shimla Baba" praying
in front of
Mt. Shivling,
Garwhal, India,
Ph. Heinz Zak.

Funeral procession,
Falesina,
Pergine Valsugana,
Trentino, Italy,
Ph. Flavio Faganello.

Butter lamps lightened
by tibetan pilgrims,
Jokang monastery,
Lhasa, Tibet,
Ph. Philippe Rebreyend.

Prayer flags,
Mt. Kangchenjunga seen
from Dzongri peak,
Himalaya, Sikkim, India,
Ph. Pat Morrow.

Ceremony for
Rimpoche reincarnation,
Lhasa, Tibet,
Ph. DC. Henriette.

Arlberg, Austrian Alps,
Ph. Peter Mathis.

Carmel du Reposoir,
Cluse-Haute Savoie,
France,
Ph. Claude Gardien.

Praying towards Mecca,
Atlas, Morocco,
Ph. Eduardo Velasco.

Meditation and
contemplation on the
summit of Mt. Granero,
Val Pellice, Italy,
Ph. Guillaume Vallot.

St. Bonnet's cemetery,
St. Bonnet,
South of Alps, France,
Ph. Guillaume Vallot.

"Christ of the
Third Millennium",
Mt. Bondone, Cima Palon,
Trentino, Italy,
Ph. Flavio Faganello.

Prayer flags
in front of Stupa,
Bhutan, India,
Ph. Gerhard Heidorn.

Painted stone circle
by Jean Verame,
Bardai oasis, Tibesti, Chad
Ph. Heinz ZaK.

Lights   *Luci*   *Lumières*   *Licht*   *Luces*

L I G H T S

Mt. Matterhorn, Zermatt,
Switzerland,
Ph. Maggiorino Michiardi.

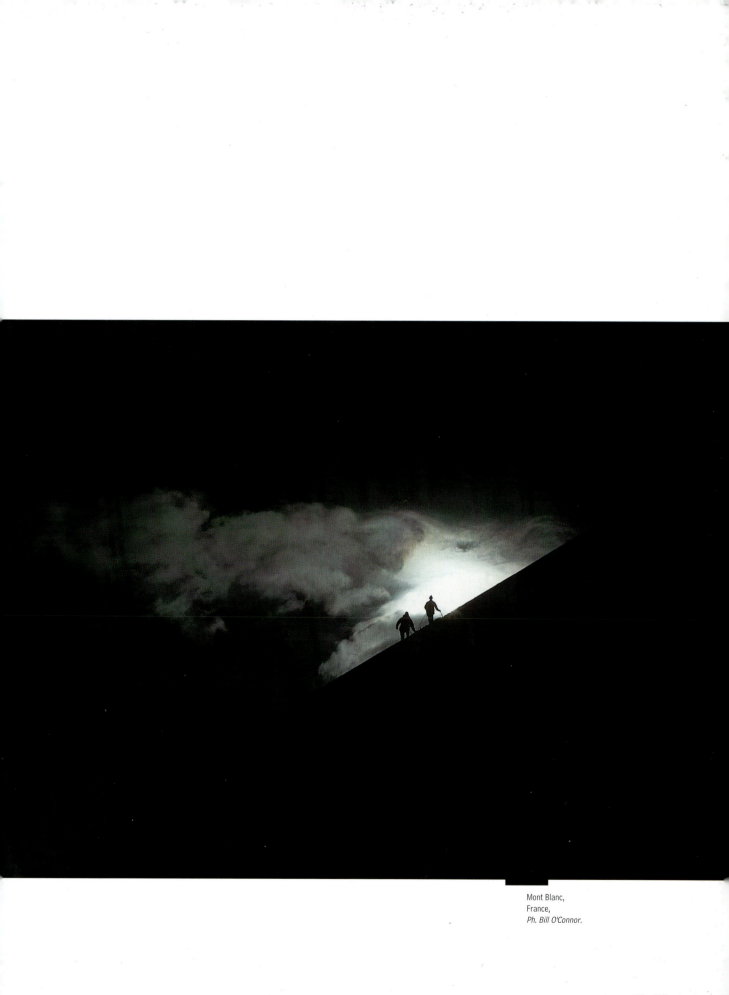

Mont Blanc,
France,
Ph. Bill O'Connor.

Westside of Alpamayo,
Peru,
Ph. Patrick Wagnon.

Hohe Kugel,
Vorarlberg, Austria,
Ph. Peter Mathis.

Khumbu Valley,
Nepal,
Ph. Laurence Gouault.

Desert of Atacama,
Andes, Chile,
Ph. Fulvio Maiani.

Tibet,
Ph. Alex Huber.

Austrian/Swiss Alps,
Ph. Dietmar Walser.

Shelfice and
Emperor penguin,
Dronning Maud Land,
Antarctica,
Ph. Anders Modig.

Mt. Testa Bernarda
seen from Varda,
Aosta Valley, Italy,
Ph. Maurizio Fonte

Glacier Vatnajökull,
Iceland,
Ph. Eduardo Velasco

Finsteraarhorn,
Bernese Oberland,
Switzerland,
Ph. Robert Bösch.

Large iceberg
(40 m lenght),
Dronning Maud Land,
Antarctica,
Ph. Anders Modig.

PHOTO EDITOR
Betta Gobbi

CONCEPT
Gioachino Gobbi

ART DIRECTOR
Eliana Barbera

DESIGNER
Rosa Malfitano

EDITOR
Marco A. Ferrari
Volker Leuchsner

PHOTOLITHOGRAPHY
Studio PRO srl, Torino

PRINTED BY
G. Canale & C. spa, Torino

Published by
Vivalda Editori srl

Yearly Publication
Pubblicazione annuale

PHOTOGRAPHERS

Sam Bié
R. Sainte Cathérine, 11
34000 Montpellier
France
Phone & Fax: 0494.842307

Jérome Blanc Gras
05380 Saint-Alban
Chateauroux les Alpes
France
E-mail: jblancgras@aol.com
Phone & Fax: 0492.451878

Gian Luca Boetti
St. Crosa, 14
10017 Montanaro (TO)
Italy
Phone & Fax: 011.9192172

Robert Bösch
Morgartenstr., 20
6315 Oberägeri
Switzerland
Phone: 041.7505755
Fax: 041.7500155
E-mail: rboesch@access.ch

Laurent Bouvet/Rapsodia
Av. Marcel Dassault, 1548
74370 Argonay (Annecy)
France
Phone: 0450.272165
Fax: 0450.271464
Web: www.rapsodia.fr

Davide Camisasca
P.zza Umberto I, 9
11025 Gressoney (AO)
Italy
Phone: 0125.355305

Simon Carter
P. O. Box 49
Blackheath
2785 New South Wales
Australia
Phone & Fax: 02.47877155
E-mail: onsight@flash.com.au

Sylvie Chappaz
Chemin de la Capuche, 15/17
38100 Grenoble
France
Phone & Fax: 0476.460898

Cesare Cossavella
Fraz. Ville, 26
11020 Arnad (AO)
Italy
Phone: 0125.969978

Daniel J. Cox/Franca Speranza
V. Melzo, 9
20129 Milano
Italy
Phone: 02.29402599
Fax: 02.29406440

Manrico Dell'Agnola
V. Farra, 130
32026 Mel (BL)
Italy
Phone e Fax: 0347.540472
E-mail: manrico@writeme.com

Sergio De Leo
V. Parigi, 22
11100 Aosta
Italy
Phone: 0165.361588
Fax: 0165.364520

Erik Decamp
Les Chavaux
74310 Les Houches
France
Phone: 0450. 545923
Fax: 0450.545924
E-mail: erik@destivelle.com

Rainer Eder
Scheffelstr., 41
8037 Zürich
Switzerland
Phone: 01.3625180

Flavio Faganello
V. Serafini, 9
38100 Trento
Italy
Phone & Fax: 0461.234539

Fengler Klaus
Blissenweg, 10a
78476 Allensbach
Germany
Phone: 07533.997419
Fax: 07531.863640
E-mail:
klaus.fengler@kst.siemens.de

Maurizio Fonte
V. Pascal
11010 Pré St. Didier
Italy
Phone: 0165.846279

Patrick Gabarrou
La Cour Agy
74300 Saint Sigismond
France
Phone & Fax: 0450.342485

Andrea Gallo/Idee Verticali
V. Gallesio, 11
17024 Finale Ligure (SV)
Italy
Phone & Fax: 019.695997

Claude Gardien
Le Martelet
74300 Chatillon
France
Phone & Fax: 0450.343818

Laurence Gouault
Chalet Touze, B. P. 32
74310 Les Houches
France
E-mail: slhaston@aol.com

Kennan Harvey
P. O. Box 882
81302 Durango, CO
U.S.A.
E-mail:
kennaneharvey@compuserve.com

Frédéric Hasbani
R. Jean Macé, 37
38000 Grenoble
France

Stevie Haston
Chalet Touze, B. P. 32
74310 Les Houches
France
E-mail: slhaston@aol.com

Gerhard Heidorn
Bucherstr., 12
87476 Oy-Mittelberg
Germany
Phone: 08361.923431
Fax: 08361.923437
E-mail: heidorn@allgaeu.org

D. C. Henriette/Franca Speranza
V. Melzo, 9
20129 Milano
Italy
Phone: 02.29402599
Fax: 02.29406440

Sauli Herva/Luonnonlaki
Activities
Kurkelantie, 1g
90230 Oulu
Finland
Phone: 0400.585317
Fax: 0855.71049

Leo Himsl/Fotostories
Schärdingerstr., 23
4910 Ried im Innkreis
Austria
Phone: 07752.71442
Fax: 07752.71443
E-mail: office@fotostories.at

Alexander Huber
Locksteinstr., 49
83471 Berchtesgaden
Germany
Phone: 08652.690990
Fax: 08652.690991

Thomas Huber
Locksteinstr., 49
83471 Berchtesgaden
Germany
Phone: 08652.690990
Fax: 08652.690991